The End of

Democracy

By Edward Benjamin

Preface

"The worst form of government..."

An oft-quoted and possibly apocryphal remark by Winston Churchill holds that democracy is the worst form of government "except for all the others." It has been cited so often and so widely that it has become a cliche and a truism accepted by almost all thinking people. Yet, overwhelmingly, the phrase is quoted solely to its second clause. Rarely is attention paid to the first.

Yet the idea that democracy is deeply and perhaps fatally flawed is immensely old, and appears in some of the most ancient discussions of political theory, most notably in Plato's *Republic*. Plato theorized that there are five stages of government through which a hypothetical polity may descend. In decreasing order of desirability, he described them as aristocracy, oligarchy, rule by the wealthy, democracy, and tyranny. As can be seen, democracy was quite low on his list.

Since the American and French revolutions, however, the democratic ideal has steadily risen in esteem, to the point that it now holds a hegemonic position in political thought. It has become, in fact, akin to a religious ideal. Democracy is held to be a good in and of itself, and all efforts at reform or revolution should be directed toward achieving it.

Since the fall of the communist bloc, moreover, democracy tempered by the welfare state and constitutional rights - what is broadly called liberal democracy - has been essentially unchallenged as both the proper and indeed expected form of government. Anything else, it is believed, constitutes tyranny and barbarism. As Fukuyama's now legendary essay put it, liberal democracy represents an end of history. It may not be the best government, but it is the best mankind is likely to come up with. Mankind's political evolution ended, in effect, in 1989.

It is my belief that this is not the case, and that even now we are seeing the collapse of liberal democracy and the emergence of a non-democratic order. Forms of government are taking shape, as the result of both conscious and unconscious forces, that are challenging the hegemony of liberal democracy and will eventually replace it. These forces are both a reaction to and a result of the inherent flaws in liberal democracy, and while there is no guarantee that they will be superior to it, there is also no guarantee that they will be worse. There appear to be two likely candidates for succession, and they are described herein as theocracy and neo-aristocracy.

I do not say with absolute certainty that liberal democratic hegemony will end, or that these regimes will be its replacements. But I think it is very likely, and that we will soon have to contend with a world in which the settled questions of politics will become unsettled, while humanity's natural tendency to seek security and stability in the cultures and polities they share with others will drive them to seek alternatives to what were once accepted certainties.

The regimes I believe will eventually replace liberal democracy will not be particularly democratic ones. Whether they will retain certain freedoms and rights that have become sacred to much of humanity is an open question. It is quite possible that readers today may find the very possibility of such regimes offensive. But it is worth pointing out that

3

mankind can and has done a great deal worse. There is the possibility that, given the economic, religious, and political crises in which much of the world is now entangled, the choice will be between the regimes I describe and forms of tyranny that will not only violate the rights of man but return him to a wretched, impotent slavery and perhaps oblivion. The options presented to us by history are rarely palatable, and it may be that the possibilities I describe are indeed very bad, except, as Churchill so famously put it, for all the others.

Introduction

The *Ancien Regime*

The heroic age of liberal democracy is coming to a close. We do not yet know what will replace it, but it is likely to be of a decidedly non-democratic nature. The proverbial Golden Mean, which since 1989 has been firmly in the possession of liberal democracy, appears to be slowly shifting elsewhere; and the underlying concepts of liberal democracy, which might well be called sacred to the societies that embrace them, will probably no longer be so. Indeed, it is not unthinkable that, a century from now, men will look back on them as the follies of a more primitive era.

The proverbial writing, as they say, is already on the wall. In today's world, democracy is coming to encompass a smaller and smaller sphere of governance. More religiously inclined societies are moving steadily toward theocracy, sometimes by way of democracy, but theocracy nonetheless. Buttressed by religious institutions and ways of life that long predate liberal democracy, they are emerging not only as a zealous ideal but as a practical alternative.

At the same time, secular nations are becoming ever more aristocratic in both politics and social organization. While this tendency has wealth as one of its expressions, it is by no means the only one. They are also moving toward aristocracies of skill, knowledge, and culture.

These changes are largely a result of liberal democracy's inbuilt flaws. It has long been noted that certain basic concepts of democracy are, upon examination, deeply problematic. The idea of *vox populi vox dei*, for example, is a clearly mystical concept with little basis in reality. The idea of majority rule has long been recognized as potentially harmful to democracy itself, given the majority's marked vulnerability to demagogic politics and its tendency to descend into mob rule. The idea of rights, while it appears to be so concrete to those who believe in it, is upon examination more akin to a mutually agreed upon illusion, similar to the institution of paper money.

At the basis of democracy is, of course, the concept of "the people" as the ultimate authority and their right to self-governance. Again, the objective observer is forced to note certain drawbacks to this approach. First, there is the amorphous concept of a right to self-governance. If the people are the ultimate authority, from where is this authority itself derived? Again, the only consistent answer would have to be God, which is not an answer at all. The only other answer is an obvious tautology: The people have the right to self-governance because they are the ultimate authority, and therefore have the authority to grant themselves the right to be the ultimate authority. This leads us nowhere, and also has distinctly religious overtones, bearing an obvious resemblances to the "First Cause" of Aristotelian theology.

On another, perhaps more serious level, liberal democracy often runs headlong into the brick wall of reality. Put simply, most human beings are not capable of governing themselves and likely never will be. If a government, whatever system it is based on, is to be capable of any degree of stability and even competence, it must be ruled by a small group of capable men, though they may seek from time to time the endorsement of the people in deference to the sacred principle of their ultimate authority.

As knowledgeable people will recognize, none of these problems are new, and many of them are quite ancient. Nonetheless, there are perhaps two arguments in favor of democracy that *are* relatively new.

First, liberal democracy has met the challenge of history and triumphed. This is an inherently problematic argument, since the human race likely has a great deal more history before it, and the triumph of a few centuries may well appear to be a brief anomaly from the perspective of millennia. It suffers as well from the fact that, when faced with crisis or challenge, democracies have nearly always resorted to more oligarchical forms of governance and, it should be noted, often achieved their greatest successes while so organized. Put simply, democracies appear to be governed better the more oligarchical they become.

The second argument is probably the strongest: The only alternative to liberal democracy is barbarism. Certainly, the history of the 20th century would seem to provide a great deal of strong evidence for this. Communism and Nazism, as well as a host of other non- or anti-democratic forms of government ran up a butcher's bill of shocking proportions between the end of World War I and the fall of the Berlin Wall, and these atrocities are, it is claimed, directly attributable to the non-democratic nature of these regimes. Therefore, goes the argument, the world is under a moral obligation to adopt democracy in order to avoid repeating such atrocities.

While this argument appears at first to be both emotionally compelling and objectively irrefutable, it is a bit more complicated than it appears. As conservative thinkers have often noted, the rise of the great tyrannies of the 20th century were enabled by democracy as much as they were hindered by it, for they were all based on political parties that were in turn based on mass movements of ordinary people. And indeed, almost all the atrocities committed by these regimes were committed in the name of the people. Most of them appeared or rose to power, moreover, as reactions to the collapse of the old order as a result of World War I. In other words, they came to power because the old, oligarchical forms of government collapsed. Had these forms survived, the situation would have been quite different.

At the same time, thinkers of the Left have pointed out that the bloody record of the totalitarian states was in many ways a product of a basic failing in liberal democracy: the failure to recognize the specific, real world depredations suffered by ethnic, racial, political, religious, economic, and other minorities within a democratic system. Whether we want to admit it or not, these critics say, in a society with equal rights, some are more equal than others, and societies must try to ameliorate or eliminate this problem. In effect, they claim, totalitarianism is simply majority rule taken to its logical extreme.

These arguments are, of course, made in the service of differing ideals, one of support for older, oligarchical forms of power (the Right) and one in favor of minority rights (the Left), but once one steps back from the political rivalries of the moment, it appears that both are quite correct.

Perhaps the most striking indication of this is that almost all of the world's liberal democracies are struggling with these issues, and their response has generally been - often without saying so explicitly - a move away from democracy toward both oligarchical institutions and forms of radical pluralism that vitiate the liberal democratic concept of equal rights.

We find, then, that in many ways the experience of the 20th century has not only taught the world the existential dangers of tyranny, but also the discontents and possibly fatal drawbacks to liberal democracy. It seems, moreover, that this is the primary reason for the increasing tendency of liberal democratic societies to move quietly but nonetheless steadily away from the principles of liberal democracy and toward different forms of political and social organization.

Having said all this, we are still left wondering what the answer will be to these various failings of liberal democracy. As noted above, the most likely response will be that liberal democracy will slowly disappear. Among the secular nations it will likely continue to evolve into what will be, in effect, a form of neo-aristocracy. Among more religious societies, the most obvious alternative is a theocratic form of government, and we are already seeing this taking shape in many parts of the world.

It is equally likely that certain societies - perhaps most - will adopt a hybrid form of government, in which theocratic elements will share power with a secular aristocracy. They may coexist in harmony or hostility, but it is unlikely that - in the absence of a violent seizure of power and the imposition of outright tyranny - that one side will be able to completely dominate the other.

These changes do not lie far in the future. In many places they have been underway for some time, and in others they are clearly on the way. More to the point, the discontents of liberal democracy are increasingly prominent, and even in those societies that have previously dealt with them in silence, they are beginning to be discussed quite openly. Liberal democracy is still seen in many parts of the world as the dominating ideology of the age, but it seems unlikely that this age will live out the century. It may well be that the end of liberal democracy will come sooner than many of us think.

I

The Magistrates of God

The theocrat's argument against democracy is a simple one: Democracy is a betrayal of God and the commandments of God. As such, it is a form of sin and blasphemy that not only endangers human happiness but also the human soul.

This appears, at first, to be an entirely irrational argument, and indeed it is; though it is not necessarily, as we have seen, any *more* irrational than many of the arguments in favor of liberal democracy. It does, however, point to two aspects of liberal democracy that its proponents often overlook. First, it is inherently unstable and insecure. Second, for all the benefits it may bring in its wake, it also accompanied by a great deal of destruction.

The first issue has long been noted. Because democracy involves, as part of its very nature, the capacity for immense change in government, laws, leadership, and even the basic order of society, it is by definition unstable. In democratic societies, which regard this potential as a form of freedom, which is in turn considered an axiomatic good, it can be difficult to comprehend how serious a flaw this actually is.

It is important to remember, then, that the primary - perhaps the only - organizing principle of any society is to provide for the security and well-being of its members. For a great many - perhaps on some level all - people, security and well-being are synonymous with stability. The world around us is indifferent and often threatening, our fellow men are often the same, and it is quite natural that people should look to their societies primary as a shield against the inevitable depredations of life. Indeed, even the most fervent advocates of liberal democracy have acknowledged that, should this basic need go unaddressed, a democratic society often falls quite easily to a tyranny that exacts freedom as the price of security and safety.

Gathering together into larger and larger groups for mutual protection is one of the ways mankind has tried to guard itself from the insecurities of the world. But one of the others - and certainly equally important and influential - has been that of religion. Where society provides for physical security, religion provide psychological security. It asserts that there is an absolute, transcendent, and immortal order to the universe; that this order is ultimately benevolent, or at least not hostile; and that adherence to the demands of this order - i.e., commandments and religious obligations - will yield benefits such as enlightenment and immortality.

Looked at in this way, the appeal of a theocratic regime should be obvious. A theocracy is a form of government that places either religious law, a clerisy, or both at the head of a society. This

12

provides not only physical stability but also psychological and social stability at the same time. For its adherents, it is literally the best of all worlds.

At the same time, a theocratic regime benefits from a simple but often overlooked fact: Democracy as a widespread phenomenon is an extremely new thing, and a product of modernity. It brings with it enormous changes not only in governance but also in entire ways of life. While there are many people from many diverse societies who believe that these changes are beneficial, it cannot be denied that they are also what the philosopher Walter Benjamin named "the storm called progress" and the French call *la rupture*. Liberal democracy, when it comes, often sweeps away older, un- or non-democratic ways of living that have lasted for centuries and whose adherents cannot imagine any other way of existing. The extreme, vertiginous sense of emptiness and anxiety that follows has been noted at many times and in many societies, and there can be no doubt that it has enormous social and political consequences.

Against this psychological void, theocracy offers the surety of its transcendent order and its sharply defined set of duties and benefits. Moreover, it is quite often derived from precisely those older religious, cultural, and social beliefs and traditions that are threatened by liberal democracy. As such, theocracy provides an answer to what is one of liberal democracy's greatest flaws: its inability to provide for certain very deep and perhaps fundamental needs of the human psyche.

Given its immense age and the enormous power religion has often wielded over most of human history, it is, in fact, remarkable how rare genuine theocracies have actually been. Even those that have existed were often tempered by secular forces that acted as a check on and often a rival to the religious leadership. Priests and clerics seem to be somehow unsuited by both temperament and training for official political leadership, and have usually been most effective as an outside influence on secular government. While many religions have enjoyed official establishment and patronage, their genuine power has rarely matched that of kings, ministers, generals, and other secular officials.

In this sense, our age appears to be quite different, as we are now seeing the ascent of "pure" theocracies and theocratic movements in many places around the world, with many more waiting in the wings for history to call upon their services.

To an extent, this has been the result of conscious internal forces within religious institutions themselves. As noted above, the artisans of religion have tended to hold themselves somewhat aloof from politics, perhaps because they lacked a talent for it, perhaps because they lacked the interest. So much of religion, after all, is about the next world, and not this one. In recent decades, however, organized religious movements and their official representatives have broken with this tradition, and have deliberately cultivated the art of practical politics. While advocating for the supremacy of religious law, they have nonetheless become as adept at navigating its secular counterpart as their non-religious rivals.

This is, in part, because of a conscious broadening of ambition on the part of theocratic movements. At a certain point, it appears, the feeling grew among certain religious movements that the next world is not enough. Their goal therefore became the acquisition of temporal - that is, political - power, followed by the reform and in many cases the complete reconstitution of their societies along religious lines. In many cases, this has meant the literal imposition of religious law on an entire polity. That is to say, it has meant the entrance of religious law into the secular realm and - in theory, at least - the erasure of the line between the secular and the religious so that the two become, in effect, indistinguishable.

As noted, this is a somewhat unprecedented event. While there have been points at which religious or quasi-religious codes of conduct carried the authority of law, there have been very few in which a modern, centralized state has come to be not only subject to religious law but also to religious *management*, so to speak. That this process bears some resemblance to the totalitarian states of the 20th century has been much noted, but it is also quite different, in that it does propose an authority beyond that of the party, the leader, or an ideology - i.e., God.

It has also been noted that this movement is reactionary and anti-modern in nature. This is also not entirely true. While theocracy is a reformist or revolutionary movement that seeks to reassert the authority of pre-modern codes of conduct and ways of life, it now seeks to do so *without* returning to pre-modern forms of social and political organization. It desires instead to replace secular modernity with something like a religious modernity, a phenomenon that is quite unprecedented and whose eventual form can only be guessed at.

While this phenomenon has been most prominent in the Islamic world, it has not been confined to it, and there is no reason to suppose that the coming theocracies will be exclusively Islamic. There is, for example, a large and largely underreported expansion of Christianity currently underway in sub-Saharan Africa. More importantly, this Christianity appears to be a strikingly orthodox variety. It bears little or no resemblance to the nominal Christianity of Europe, for example, which has made a valiant but probably doomed attempt over the last century to slough off the more furious aspects of the ancient faith while retaining its more pastoral and ecumenical ideals, rendering everything else unto Caesar.

Already, this has caused an official schism between the Church of England and its more theocratically inclined congregations, and it seems likely that further such splits are all but inevitable. Christianity has always had a singular talent for sectarianism, and where once the debates were over the nature of Christ, they are now over what is, essentially, the issue of religion in a liberal democratic society.

This split in what was once referred to as Christendom is an excellent illustration of the growth of theocratic forces within an established religion. Liberal Christians are largely in favor of a what is, in historical terms, a highly truncated role for Christianity in the larger society. This is in keeping with liberal democratic values of tolerance and religious freedom, and especially with its strongly anticlerical tendencies. Authority in liberal democracies is - so goes the shibboleth - derived from the people and not from God, and therefore God must serve the people and not vice versa.

It is precisely this that Christianity's emerging theocrats reject. Since God is the final source of authority, a society must conform to his laws and commandments, and if these contradict liberal democracy, it is liberal democracy that must yield, and not vice-versa.

One sees this quite clearly in regard to "hot-button" issues such as abortion and homosexual rights. Europe's liberal Christians, in supporting homosexual rights, for example, have decided that the values of liberal democracy must win out over religious law. Their opponents hold precisely the opposite. Neither of them are likely to give an inch on this or other issues, but given the growing demographic power of the theocratic party, it seems likely that the liberals will have to resort to very illiberal methods in order to prevail.

Both sides of the argument, however, often fail to perceive a very important point: The theocratic tendencies at work in today's world - in which liberal democracy is supposedly the prevalent and in some ways only viable ideology available - are not in any meaningful sense *more religious* than their liberal or secular counterparts. As noted above, liberal democracy itself rests on foundations that can only be rationally regarded as religious in nature. In effect, liberal democracy removed the old established religions and replaced them with a civic religion; one that is quite similar to those that underlay the Athenian democracy and the Roman republic. In those societies, as in ours, politics was not just a matter for men, but also a matter for the gods.

It may well be, then, that the rise of a particular form of modern theocracy is an inevitable outcome of a basic contradiction at the heart of liberal democracy: It is a system that not only can be but must be religious and secular *simultaneously*. On the one hand, it cannot permit the establishment of clerical institutions that might challenge the ultimate sovereignty of the people. On the other hand, the only way to justify that sovereignty is through a fundamentally religious idea. *Vox populi vox dei* is not in fact an axiom but a terrible and perhaps unsolvable conundrum.

We have recently seen this contradiction acted out on the world stage in extremely dramatic fashion, with the wave of social and political change across the Middle East that has come to be called the "Arab spring." As many noted both before, during, and after the mass protests swept across the Arab world, the most likely winners of these struggles would not be liberal democrats but Islamic theocrats. Though the jury is still out to some degree, and the theocrats have not been universally successful - the liberals appear to have been victorious in Libya, for example - for the most part these predictions were proven correct.

It is easy enough to use this fact as a judgment on the Arab Spring and on the Arab world in general; but this is somewhat overly simplistic. While the electoral victories won by the forces of Islamic theocracy are unquestionable, it is worthwhile to remember that they have not violated the most essential principle of liberal democracy: *vox populi vox dei*. The people of these countries wanted Islamic rule, and when given the chance, they voted for it. Thus far, only Iran - which predates the Arab Spring by more than three decades - appears to have moved from theocracy into what can be fairly called a full-fledged religious tyranny.

This does not mean that the theocratic parties in the Arab world are not a threat to liberal democracy. They most certainly are. But this also implies that liberal democracy is in and of itself a value, that its existence constitutes, as it were, a baseline for human governance. It asserts that the proverbial Golden Mean lies with liberal democracy, and deviations from it in one direction or the other constitute a violation of both reason and rectitude.

But this is not the case. Liberal democracy can legitimately be viewed as a good form of government, perhaps the best. Certainly it is not the most pernicious. But it is not a transcendent, axiomatic good. At the same time, in order to exist at all, it must *believe* that it is a transcendent, axiomatic good. It should not be surprising that, to many people around the world, liberal democracy seems to be little more than a theocracy without a God; which is, needless to say, not a particularly appealing prospect.

It is also far too easy to confine the theocratic phenomenon to what is colloquially referred to as the Third World. There are also strong tendencies in a theocratic direction in the secular West. Besides liberal Christianity, there are the innumerable syncretist cults and New Age religions which are, lest we forget, immensely widespread and popular. At the same time, the fascination with Asian religions such as Buddhism and a fetishization of indigenous rituals of all kinds indicate a barely repressed desire for theocracy that, if spoken, would undoubtedly be violently denied by its adherents.

Nor can the role of Christianity in the United States be overlooked. Of all the secular republics of the West, America is undoubtedly the most openly torn by the discontents of liberal democracy - perhaps because it has the strongest moral and emotional feelings toward it - and its religion is no exception. Its dominating faith is essentially split in two between European-style liberal Christianity and a deeply fervent Protestantism which is in many ways similar to the resurgent Christianity of sub-Saharan Africa.

But America also illustrates the crisis of liberal democracy in that *both* of these forms of Christianity have profoundly theocratic tendencies. On one side, there is the prophetic reformism epitomized by Martin Luther King, Jr., while on the other, there is the public moralism of evangelical Christianity. They have a great deal more in common than either will admit. First, they believe that American liberal democracy rests on fundamentally religious foundations. Second, that American public life, law, and government must ultimately answer *not* to the written law of the land but to those religious values. Third, that the role of the religious person is not simply to think, worship, or speak, but to *actively agitate* for conformity to these values. Fourth, and this cannot be understated, they are prepared to see liberal democracy and even the republic itself fall into instability and violence rather than allow these values to remain unfulfilled.

The American Civil War was obviously the most bloody confrontation between the forces of theocracy and contemporary social, economic, and political realities. But it was by no means the first or last, and it often seems that the question is not when the United States will again be confronted with theocratic forces, but rather from which side the inevitable attack will come.

If theocracy is indeed growing in power and influence, and is destined to replace liberal democracy in large parts of the world, it is worth asking what form these emergent theocracies are likely to take.

First, it is very unlikely that they will be composed entirely of clerics or clerical authorities. Because the modern state requires, to some degree at least, a bureaucratic and administrative mechanism, which usually makes up the majority of the public sector of any given society, any modern theocracy will require a large and potentially powerful technocratic class in order to fulfill its most basic responsibilities. It is reasonable to suppose, then, that the majority of these theocracies, while they may not adopt its more repressive methods, will probably be similar to the Islamic regime in Iran. That is, it will be a modern, technocratic state in which ultimate authority is vested in holy writ as interpreted by a panel of clerics who are not selected by any democratic criteria.

It is less likely, however, that the emerging theocracies will adopt the Iranian regime's methods and institutions of oppression. These are unmistakably drawn from the legacy of totalitarianism, and are readily recognizable: A one-party state with its own military and secret police separate from that of the larger society. Other theocracies may well find such methods decidedly foreign and, more importantly, they may not be necessary. Iran, one should remember, was (and in many ways still is) a very secular country. As a result, its theocracy has been forced to maintain itself largely through violence. While it likely enjoyed a certain degree of general consent during the Iran-Iraq War, in the absence of an existential threat it has fallen back on cruder and more brutal means of governance; most especially the assiduous cultivation of external enemies.

This is not the case in other emerging theocracies. In countries such as Egypt, the majority of the population is quite sympathetic to religion and to theocratic values. They have voted for it without coercion of any kind, and it is unlikely that any will be required to keep such a regime in power. It may be that the government will oscillate between more or less theocracy, but barring a major cultural shift on the part of the general population (which is not likely but hardly impossible), it will not be disestablished.

In the Middle East, theocracy is easily analyzed because it is so public and its adherents openly declare it. This is not the case in other parts of the world, where theocracy may well rise to power in a quiet and perhaps entirely unspoken fashion. Indeed, even its partisans may be unaware of the actual nature of their methods and beliefs.

Should theocracy rise in the Western nations, for example, it will likely do so in just such a fashion. As unlikely as it may seem at first glance, there is no reason to believe that these nations are immune to theocracy, or that its rise is impossible due to legal or constitutional strictures on it. While the New Age and sectarian cults that are so popular in the West have yet to reach a degree of popularity and organization that would allow them to become a political force unto themselves, there is no immediate reason that they could not eventually do so. A New Age theocracy may appear absurd at first glance, but it ought to be remembered that Christianity was once an obscure cult imported from the exotic East, based around the bizarre tale of a resurrected savior. Within a few centuries, however, it dominated the Roman empire and stands today as the largest religion in the world. Even historians often forget that things which are unthinkable in the short term become normal, even banal, in the long term.

It is more likely, however, that theocracy will come from the various sects of Christianity. It will be faced, of course, with the various strictures mentioned above, in particular the constitutional limits on religion adopted by liberal democracy and its traditional anti-clericalism. Nonetheless, a theocratic movement of limited aims could legally gain political power, particularly if it enjoyed widespread popular support. It is more likely, however, that theocracy will rise like the British Empire: in a fit of absence of mind. There is no legal prohibition on clerics running for political office in any of the liberal democracies, and it is entirely possible that a cleric could, for example, be elected president of the United States, appoint a cabinet of clerics, be supported by a party led by clerics, and pursue essentially theocratic policies. While this would inevitably face a serious challenge from the secular legal system, so long as it is based on a durable shift in the culture of the majority, it would eventually and inevitably survive, particularly if the only other option were outright civil war. Even if civil war were to come, so long as theocracy commands the support of its surrounding culture, it would likely win out even in an armed confrontation. This appears to be precisely what is taking place in today's Turkey.

Should a theocratic movement manage to retain a degree of modesty as to its aims, however, whether in the West or elsewhere, it is possible that a hybrid regime will emerge. Because it would need mass support to survive in an otherwise hostile system, the theocracy would likely control the positions in government most susceptible - ironically - to democratic influence, i.e., the executive and legislative institutions of government. Secular forces, however, would likely prevail in judicial institutions and the bureaucracy, where lengthy secular education and training are necessary.

With equal irony, a theocratic regime may *require* secular forces in order to survive. Religious learning and practice also require lengthy education, and those educated in this manner usually have to forgo the acquisition of more secular skills - precisely those that are required in order to maintain a viable technocratic class and a modern economy. While secular and religious forces in a hybrid regime would likely regard each other as mortal enemies, in practice they would be codependent. Secular forces would require the theocracy in order to gain mass legitimacy, and religious forces would require the unique skills of their secular counterparts in order to maintain competent governance and general prosperity.

It is possible that we are seeing an example of the development of such a hybrid regime in the modern State of Israel. While the country defines itself as secular, it has powerful institutions of religion, and the religious population is growing faster than its secular counterpart. Many Israelis fear that, once a religious majority emerges, the country will fall to an Iranian-style theocratic tyranny. While this is possible, it is far more likely that a regime such as the one described above will take shape. Religious parties will enjoy widespread popular support, but because their closed and often entirely religious education will leave them unable to properly govern a modern state with serious economic and military challenges that cannot be addressed through religious law, they will be largely dependent on the secular classes in order to govern. It may well be that, in the future, Israel will have a government headed by rabbis but a society dominated by academic, scientific, military, and economic institutions ruled by an aggressive secular minority that cannot be dislodged without inviting disaster. It is entirely possible that a similar regime will emerge in Egypt, and perhaps eventually in Syria as well.

This issue of the necessary role of the technocratic classes is of immense importance, and not only to theocratic or potentially theocratic regimes. Even in entirely secular societies, the institutions of liberal democracy are finding themselves more and more strained by their inherent flaws and contradictions, and what is emerging to address them is a form of government that is quite different and in many ways antithetical to the liberal democracy that finds them nonetheless essential. It is very likely that this nascent regime will greatly expand its power over the coming decades, and eventually replace liberal democracy entirely. It is by no means a new form of government, and in a sense it comes with the recommendation of many of history's greatest political and moral philosophers. It is what can only be called a new aristocracy.

II

The New Aristocracy

It is necessary to begin by saying that the term aristocracy as it is used here is not the same as that employed in colloquial language. Over time, probably under the influence of English institutions, the term aristocracy has tended to describe rule by the wealthiest classes of society. This is not the meaning of the term as it is used here. It is used instead in its original meaning, as employed in ancient Greek political thought, where it simply meant "rule by the best."

As thinkers such as Aristotle and Plato pointed out, the "best" are by not necessarily the most wealthy. Plato in fact placed rule by the wealthy in the middle of his scale of political decadence. They were referring, instead, to something more akin to the modern term "meritocracy." Quite literally, the "best" were the best in the most prosaic and simple meaning of the term; i.e., those who are most intelligent, most learned, most moral, most courageous, and so on.

In making this recommendation, the ancients noted two things: First, that the best become the best by a combination of virtues, and not as the result of excellence in any one field. And second, that democracy is singularly inept at bringing such people to power. In fact, it is noticeably hostile to them, and with the exception of tyranny, democracy is the system most likely to bring the worst to power, and to allow them to conduct themselves accordingly without much impediment.

Plato was speaking, of course, of a political ideal, and Aristotle was adept at pointing out the practical flaws in many of his theories. But they largely agreed that an aristocratic government would be the best form of government, particularly if the aristocrats involved were consciously guided by the lessons of philosophy.

It may well be that, some two millennia after these two men sparred over the issue, something very much like their ideal is taking shape. This does not mean that a utopia or superior form of government is emerging, merely that a form of political organization somewhat similar to the classic concept of aristocracy appears to be doing so. That is to say, the new aristocracy may not in fact be composed of genuine aristocrats ("the best"), but they organize and conduct themselves as a genuine aristocracy would do.

Commentators have noted for some time that the birth and development of the modern, centralized, technocratic state inevitably creates a new technocratic class; a vast public sector made up of people specially trained for and perhaps temperamentally suited to such a profession. It is, essentially, a species of permanent government. The ruling parties may shift and change, but the great leviathan, the mechanism of government itself and the people who administer it, do not.

To a surprising extent, the great debates and political rivalries that have typified the history of liberal democracies have been about precisely what to do with this class. Advocates have noted that such a class is essential in order to ensure the continued stability and functioning of society, and that , properly used, its talents can lead to enormous benefits for all. The American space program, for example, the New Deal, and the socialized health and educational systems of Europe are held up as examples of this. Detractors have pointed out that a class inevitably develops interests of its own, foremost among them the desire to maintain itself in power and retain its historical privileges; and these interests may well contradict those of the larger population or the nation-state that employs them. Free market advocates such as Friedrich Hayek have even gone so far as to claim that such a class is essentially useless and redundant, because modern society is simply too complex to be governed by anything other than impersonal, automatic market forces. Such critics hold up the failure of Britain's mixed economy and especially the plodding economies of the centrally-planned Cold War socialist states as evidence of this.

Both or neither of these claims may be partially true, but they do not change the fact that such a class exists and is not going away. The modern liberal democracies have, out of necessity, created large and powerful institutions of governance *that are not accountable to the democracy they serve*. It is in the nature of these institutions to be unelected and largely autonomous in their conduct; yet they wield enormous and perhaps decisive power over the societies in which they exist.

In the most developed and complex states, and even in many that are not, these institutions of government are intertwined in innumerable ways with non-governmental institutions that are equally autonomous and unaccountable to any democratic system: Universities, scientific laboratories, think tanks, non-governmental organizations, and - perhaps most importantly - all manner of corporate persons, from the standard business corporation to the average rotary club. Though the relationships between these groups are so byzantine as to be essentially incomprehensible, their activities usually unnoticed, and the codes of conduct they respect almost always unwritten and often unspoken, no modern society can function without them. If only because they are usually the most educated, the most competent, the best qualified, and often the most intelligent and gifted members of society.

The partisan of liberal democracy has a visceral negative reaction to this, but this is not necessarily justified. If the neo-aristocracy is composed of qualified, able, moral, and honest men - as Plato and Aristotle hoped it would be - there is no reason to think that it will be a negative influence on society. But this is no argument against the fact that these institutions fundamentally contradict the most basic founding principles of liberal democracy. *Vox populi* in this case is most certainly not *vox dei*. In fact, the voice of the people might as well not exist at all. Yet to dispense with these institutions would render any society - liberal, democratic, or otherwise - mired in impotent anarchy.

The importance of these institutions has been growing for well over a century, and even the wave of neoliberalism that dominated the Anglophone world for the last several decades in fact did little to dislodge it - a source of endless frustration for partisans of neoliberalism. It is, ironically, somewhat *because* of this brief triumph of neoliberalism that this class is becoming a decisive factor. With the massive expansion of the global economy, the profound dynamic instability of modern hyper-capitalism came to be a fact of life for almost everyone in the developed world. While technocratic institutions may sometimes - as Hayek pointed out quite rightly - be slow to react to the dizzying pace of change in modern societies, they are nowhere near as slow as elected democratic institutions. During the latest economic crisis, it has been widely noted that the executives and legislators of the developed world have proven to be not so much inept as overwhelmed by the pace of developments. They plod along behind while the fire races ahead.

In such a situation, where market forces of immense speed and power appear to be uncontrollable and the traditional institutions of democratic governance find themselves unable to cope, society may reach what is essentially a state of anarchy. The possible consequences of this are obvious, and we have already seen some of the results in Spain and Greece, both in terms of a crisis that reaches well beyond economics into social and political realms, and in terms of open violence in the streets.

The only available stabilizing force in such a situation has already been revealed to us in countries like Italy, in which the technocratic class has filled the vacuum of power. Even more telling is the fact that, for the most part, the new technocratic governments have not been elected but installed by equally technocratic national and transnational institutions.

This development, again, sends chills down the spine of the partisan of liberal democracy, but it is a perfectly reasonable action to take. When society is in a crisis of a specific nature, it makes a great deal of sense to hand over control to people who specialize in handling such things. To hand it over to the average voter or, worse still, to rioters and radicals, makes no sense whatsoever, and would obviously invite further disaster.

In all likelihood, this is the reason such technocratic regimes - whether temporary or permanent - will probably prove to be the wave of the future in the developed, secular nation-states. They will be, quite simply, the only competent source of stability, security, and effective governance in societies otherwise mired in a state of permanent chaos and crisis. For various reasons, mainly technological, globalization is very unlikely to recede despite the economic crisis, and will probably grow even more dynamic, unpredictable, and uncontrollable. As it does so, the institutions of liberal democracy will become ever more ritualized and hollow, while real power is invested in the technocratic class, which will serve as the proverbial eye of the storm to which society can retreat for both day-to-day stability and open intervention in moments of crisis.

Putting aside the issue of economics, another factor is equally important in weakening liberal democracy and strengthening the technocratic class. It is, put simply, the feudalization of modern society. Whereas liberal democracy is predicated on the idea of "the people" as a single corporate being representing a single will, the emerging neo-feudalism is based on the idea of society as an agglomeration of autonomous groups, defined by all manner of various social and cultural identities, enjoying different and specific rights and privileges.

This system emerged largely as an attempt to redress the shortcomings of liberal democracy in regard to the security, happiness, and freedom of minority groups. Yet these challenges were not simply malfunctions, but a direct result of certain fatal contradictions inherent in liberal democracy; most especially, the centrality of an undifferentiated people and an undifferentiated individual. In practice, of course, all people belong to certain groups, voluntarily or otherwise; these groups are rarely equal in terms of numbers, power, wealth, etc.; and to accord them all identical rights and privileges will inevitably benefit some and harm others.

The result, as conservatives have bemoaned and liberals have applauded, is a society that has been vaguely called multicultural but is in fact much closer to the feudal societies of medieval Europe. It is one in which racial, religious, sexual, ethnic, and innumerable other minorities are part of what in America is termed an "identity politics," in which an individual's membership in one or many of these groups defines the rights and privileges he enjoys.

Both proponents and opponents of neo-feudalism have noted that it contradicts the principles of liberal democracy; the difference lies only in whether they approve or disapprove of this. The reasons should be fairly obvious. First, it demolishes the idea of "the people" by openly and officially splitting the people into various autonomous groups. Second, it vitiates the principle of equality and equal treatment under the law in that it defines these groups *in* law and grants them rights and privileges that are peculiar to them. Most importantly, it explicitly acknowledges the fact that the ideals of the people and of equality are articles of faith invoked by a civic religion, and cannot be successfully applied in reality.

What we find now in many developed nations, then, is a society that is composed of a web of semi-autonomous groups, bound together economically and socially, but not in any sense a "people," let alone a corporate person capable of a single will and speaking in a single voice. We have not the voice of the people but the voices of peoples. The recognition of the rights of minorities is swiftly reaching a point at which everyone is a minority, and the majority that a democracy requires in order to rule no longer exists.

In such a situation, the institutions of liberal democracy can at best attempt to negotiate the often dizzying web of values and interests presented by such a situation. For the most part, this involves intense and often violent competition between the representatives of these various groups, and a continuous struggle for gaining and maintaining their autonomy and the various rights derived from it.

Because this negotiation is often completely impossible to achieve in the chaos of a democratic setting, the administration of this developing neo-feudalist system has fallen overwhelmingly upon the technocratic class; in particular, on the government bureaucracy and the legal system. As neo-feudalism solidifies and becomes less and less controversial as more and more groups are recognized and receive their autonomous rights and privileges, we are likely to see the institutions of liberal democracy all but entirely withdraw from the societies they serve, and spend their energies largely on those few issues that maintain some measure of general social consensus. In all likelihood, the two most important of these will be to maintain the neo-feudalist system and to dispense the monies required in order to maintain the technocratic class that administers it. Even this, one imagines, will eventually become little more than a ritual to be enacted on a semi-annual basis. At that point, liberal democracy will have finally dispensed with all pretense of being anything other than a civic religion whose god is the rubber-stamp.

That this emerging form of government - a neo-feudalist society ruled by a technocratic overclass - is neither liberal nor democratic should be obvious. It is not at all clear, however, that it is also bad. Certainly, several advantages present themselves.

First, it acknowledges certain basic realities of human life that liberal democracy denies: The importance of autonomous identity groups, the inherent contradiction between stability and the democratic system, the non-existence of a single people with a single will, the problematic nature of majority rule, and so on.

Second, it may place in positions of power men who are superior to those who would rise in a democracy. If the technocratic class organizes itself along lines of nepotism or cronyism, this will of course not be the case. But if it on the whole does so along meritocratic lines, if it cultivates and requires of its members virtues such as knowledge, prudence, intelligence, honesty, courage, etc., and if it lays down mechanisms for the entrance and advancement of talented people while penalizing or expelling the corrupt and the incompetent, there is no reason to believe that it will be in any way inferior to its predecessor, and possibly a great deal more than that. It would indeed be a new aristocracy.

The natural objection to this is that it is wishful thinking. No ruling class that is unaccountable to the people - or anyone else - can avoid becoming corrupted. This is true, though it does not in any way address the failures of liberal democracy itself; which is just as, if not more likely to be corrupted, albeit in a different way.

It is unlikely, moreover, that there will be no checks on the power of the new aristocracy. The very complexity of its makeup will provide something of a check. To invoke the parallel to feudalism once again, the checks and balances that once existed between the monarchy, the Church, and the various professional guilds will reproduce itself in a much more complex and diverse form.

Indeed, the primary threat to the neo-aristocracies will not be its own corruption but the same threat that has bedeviled such regimes throughout history: a revolt of the underclass. Competent and even exemplary government is often not popular government, and the discontents occasioned by the mere existence of social hierarchy of any kind are profound and unavoidable. There will be, moreover, the persistent memory of liberal democracy and even the enactment of its rituals, all of which will serve as a perpetual reminder of less-controlling if also less secure forms of government.

The very competence of the neo-aristocracy will likely also be a source of friction, in that it is usually at the point when a certain degree of social stability and prosperity have been achieved that larger discontents begin to emerge. When people no longer have to struggle to feed and protect themselves, other ambitions come to fore.

A revolt, violent or otherwise, by the underclass also brings with it the possibility of debasing the neo-aristocracy itself. Faced with possible chaos and a fall from power, the neo-aristocrats may well resort to measures that will eventually cause a descent into an oligarchical tyranny in which the former aristocrats rule by violence rather than by virtue of their skills. If the neo-aristocracy does not pay copious attention to the maintenance and cultivation of its virtues, such an outcome will be inevitable.

In order for the new aristocracy to emerge as the hegemonic authority in any given society, that society must be largely without the theocratic tendencies that will be the neo-aristocracy's principal rival. This fact will likely render the standard paradigms of "East vs. West" and "First vs. Third World" irrelevant. While secular Europe has already emerged as a likely candidate for neo-aristocracy - and in that it is simply resurrecting its ancient traditions - it is equally likely that neo-aristocracy will be the hegemonic regime in the nations of Asia and the Pacific Rim. While countries such as China, Japan, Singapore, Thailand, and others have venerable religious traditions, they do not appear to have theocratic tendencies, perhaps because they are not monotheist in nature, perhaps because religion is so tightly intertwined with other institutions like the family that it cannot emerge as a separate political movement.

Nor, though many of them now have institutions of liberal democracy, do these nations have any long history of or moral investment in the liberal democratic tradition. Countries like China and Singapore openly reject liberal democracy to a greater or lesser degree, and Singapore has proposed the separate paradigm of communitarianism, based largely on Confucian thought.

It may be, however, that the primary model for the emerging aristocracies will be Japan. While it has been governed by a nominal liberal democracy since the end of World War II, in practice it is governed by a neo-aristocratic web of institutions that includes everything from corporate CEOs to government bureaucrats to organized crime.

While it is common to point out the flaws in this system, it is perhaps more informative to note its extraordinary success: It has succeeded in modernizing Japan while retaining its indigenous culture and social fabric, resurrected its country from near-complete destruction in war, and fostered a degree of political stability unknown in the West. While there have often been violent clashes between the far-Left and Right, the vast Center ruled by the aristocracy has scarcely noticed them, and remains nearly identical to its initial post-World War II form.

Many critics of the Japanese system note that the country's economy has been largely stagnant for two decades, and is plagued by problems of youth unemployment and a low birth rate. This is indeed true, though it is not necessarily a fatal flaw. Japan is stagnant but stable, which cannot be said of the liberal democracies of the West and even Japan's more democratic neighbors. It has avoided economic collapse in the recent crisis, and once the enormous bulge in the population that resulted from the Baby Boom passes from the scene, many of its problems with unemployment and public debt will do so as well. The transition will be difficult, but hardly on the scale of, for example, the post-World War II shift away from a military tyranny, which Japan managed to navigate with great success.

The question remains, however, of how the neo-aristocracies will act on an international level, and how they will organize the intensely globalized world in which they will inevitably exist. Perhaps more importantly, how will they relate to the emergent theocracies and various hybrid regimes on their borders, and how will these rivals relate to them?

III

Tranquility or Apocalypse?

What kind of world will be made by these emerging regimes? How will theocracy and neo-aristocracy reform the international system on which the peace and economy of the globe now depend?

The most likely prospect for the neo-aristocracies is a realm of hegemony dominated by the East Asian countries, with a rump Europe and some of the countries of North and South America making up the rest. It will probably be dominated by China and Japan, and to a lesser extent, Singapore. The Europeans will find their influence sharply truncated, but they will probably find this a small price to pay for a way out of their current state of crisis. Whether the European Union will survive the transition is in question, but the new aristocracy is morally dedicated to it, and will not give up on it easily. Nonetheless, as the new aristocracy emerges as the hegemonic regime, the EU will probably shrink in influence until it is essentially a mechanism, a minor cog in a much larger machine.

The same will likely happen to international institutions like the UN. It will survive as a useful tool, but will be become more and more of a debating society than it already is, split down the middle between the new aristocracies and the emerging theocracies; while its vast army of bureaucrats will be essentially absorbed into their respective hegemonic regimes.

There will probably be some kind of Asian EU, vastly more powerful than its European counterpart, encompassing the neo-aristocracies of East Asia. Given the superior economic potential of aristocracy, it will probably dominate a hostile theocratic bloc that will emerge in opposition to it.

In all likelihood, the neo-aristocratic bloc will not include the United States. Given its theocratic tendencies and its moral investment in the concepts of liberty and independence, as well as the staunch pride usually maintained by a fallen hegemon, it will remain on the periphery of the neo-aristocratic bloc rather than its theocratic rival, as its aristocratic elements will likely dominate, as they do now, America's economic and bureaucratic institutions. Foreign policy is usually a bureaucrats' realm, and they will be extremely unwilling to bind themselves to a theocratic bloc that is so similar to their own domestic rivals.

The theocracies will, despite the obstacles presented by their form of government, preside over a vast area and large populations. As many have already predicted, it seems likely that they will dominate most of the Middle East, the Muslim republics of the former Soviet Union and Turkey, and parts of the Indian subcontinent, especially Pakistan. It is also likely, however, that theocracy will enjoy considerable success in North and sub-Saharan Africa, where a resurgent and militant Christianity is already emerging as a decisive force in otherwise chaotic societies.

Religious forms of social organization lend themselves to high birth rates, and in the realm of demographics the theocracies will likely overwhelm the neo-aristocracies. These large populations will also be mostly homogeneous, as religious minorities flee to the neo-aristocracies or convert in order to advance themselves in the larger society. Those that remain will probably retain a certain degree of autonomy that encompasses both unique rights and unique oppressions.

The theocracies will therefore be able to wield a force of immense power in the form of their large and homogeneous populations. These nations will be unified under a single God with a single set of social mores, expectations, and restrictions. Consensus will likely rule, as will not be the case in many of the neo-aristocracies, with their intricate webs of competing groups and institutions.

At the same time, however, this enormous population will put great strain on theocratic societies. Because they will be handicapped by religion's inevitable emphasis on the next world, as well as the basic impracticalities of religious life, their economic development will be highly truncated, and a situation of widespread poverty will likely exist. Nonetheless, this poverty will be shared by all, and will therefore serve to unify more than to divide. Certainly, the theocracies will be much more egalitarian and less hierarchical than their neo-aristocratic counterparts.

There is also the persistent danger of descent into the type of repression and oppression that are embodied in the Iranian tyranny. Religion, particularly once it takes political power, can justify an enormous number of horrors, and while the most likely targets will be those religious minorities that have not already fled, there is always the possibility that the theocratic regimes will become more and more draconian in their methods.

This will not necessarily be the case, however. A great deal of modern religious extremism is a reaction to secular modernity. In the event of a viable theocracy, religious strictures may well moderate as the religious authorities feel themselves to be less and less threatened by the temptations of secular modernity. Indeed, this would be in many ways a return to the more traditional forms of religious life. Islam, as many have noted, was often a moderate faith, observed more as a way of life than a fervent set of ideological beliefs.

The most dangerous domestic threat to the theocratic bloc will, of course, be that of sectarianism and schism, and with it internecine war. The divisions between Sunni, Shia, and Sufi forms of Islam have been an object of much comment recently, and Christianity's struggles with itself have been famously brutal. The rise of theocracy may put an end to certain divisions, but it will raise up new ones that may prove to be more devastating than their secular counterparts. Where the neo-aristocracies will be united by the shared interests of their overclasses, the theocracies will be frequently torn apart by forces entirely unconcerned with the circumstances of the material world.

The role that hybrid regimes will play in this new order is the most difficult to predict. They will be more geographically scattered and less internally and externally unified than the hegemonic regimes. It is possible that they will take a place similar to that of the non-aligned nations of the Third World during the Cold War, swinging back and forth between the camps or playing the two off each other to serve their own interests.

Obviously, the primary determining factor in this will be the extent to which theocracy and neo-aristocracy influence a particular society. Those nations in which strong theocratic forces are at work will probably lean toward the theocratic bloc, and vice-versa. Competing forces may have distinctly counterintuitive results, however. India, for example, will likely be a hybrid regime (though a Hindu theocracy is by no means unthinkable), but it's fraught relationship with Islam and its avowedly secular political system may well push it toward the neo-aristocracies. At the same time, the longstanding rivalry between the secular classes and the more theocratically inclined Hindu nationalists may push India in different directions at different times. Ironically, secular forces may be more inclined to align with the nearby Islamic theocracies due to the Hindu nationalists' deep opposition to Islamic influence. At the same time, they may incline toward the neo-aristocracies in order to maintain the status quo and avoid giving the Hindu nationalists' a *casus belli*.

It is quite possible that the most decisive factor may simply be location. Those hybrid regimes that are geographically close to one hegemon or another may well incline toward them simply to avoid trouble. Given that these societies are likely to be deeply divided within themselves, avoiding outside trouble will probably be a major priority for the ruling classes.

It may be that the wild card in the international system will be sub-Saharan Africa. Many of its nations are failed states or approaching such a situation, and even those that are not are in such a state of social and economic change that their eventual form cannot be guessed at. States such as Botswana and South Africa, for example, may be headed toward neo-aristocracy, while chaotic nations such as Zimbabwe may adopt a Christian or local tribal theocracy.

Africa will probably be further complicated by outside influence. The hegemonic blocs will undoubtedly see the highly unstable situation in many African countries as an opportunity for expanding their power. The theocracies will undoubtedly do so partly out of missionary zeal, while the neo-aristocracies will do so out of their desire for economic influence and a realist approach to international politics. It is unlikely that either of these will be of much benefit to Africa itself. As in the Cold War, much of Africa is likely to be either a pawn in a chess game or an object of indifferent pity.

This divided world, dominated by hegemons both theocratic and neo-aristocratic, with a non-aligned minority of hybrid regimes, could theoretically be more stable, peaceful, and indeed prosperous than the current international system. But there is one realm that has yet to be addressed. This is, of course, the question of war, and there is a strong possibility that the emerging international order will be one in which war and the threat of war will remain largely unchanged. While usually avoided, it will remain a temptation with the potential to demolish the international system entirely. Men have predicted the end of war since the invention of war. It has never come, and it is highly improbable that it ever will. Mankind has a distinct talent for it, and while these regimes will be more internally stable and probably peaceful than their liberal democratic or tyrannical predecessors, they will be deeply divided on the international stage, and the temptations to war may be all the stronger because of the general state of peace.

Both sides - the theocratic and the neo-aristocratic - will have different advantages in a military confrontation, and these advantages will in and of themselves serve as temptations. The theocracies will have the intense passions of self-sacrifice occasioned by belief in a transcendent order, and the neo-aristocracies may be tempted to war by the simple fact that they are so good at it. The organizational and technological skills of technocratic institutions are never so effective as in a state of military confrontation. The history of the last century has borne this out so well that it hardly needs mentioning.

The urge toward war on the part of the theocracies is easy enough to understand, since religious war and missionary violence are immensely old and remarkably common. In our time, Islam is notably bellicose, and Christian militias in Africa have proven to be much the same. As these competing monotheisms will likely compose the majority of the theocratic bloc, the temptation to embark on a crusade of some kind against the non-theocratic nations will be very strong.

There will also be economic and social factors that favor war. Given their large and poor populations, the pursuit of natural resources and access to new sources of wealth will be a major concern to theocratic regimes. At the same time, when they are faced, as they inevitably will be at some point, with domestic religious schism or heresy, the desire for a foreign conflict that might transcend such conflicts will be extremely strong.

This may be exacerbated by the fact that many of these regimes will almost certainly possess nuclear and other non-conventional weapons. Protected by a nuclear shield and relatively unconcerned with the possible consequences in this world, the theocracies may prove to be noticeably adventurous.

The urge will be tempered, however, by the neo-aristocracies' economic and technological superiority. It is already possible to fight a war almost entirely with air power and unmanned weapons, and these devices will only become more sophisticated and plentiful as time goes on. The neo-aristocracies will therefore be free to commit themselves to war without risking immense loss of life. At the same time, such methods will nullify the theocracies' most potent weapon, which is obviously their vast manpower and the ability of religion to transcend earthly fears of death.

Should the neo-aristocracies' find themselves in a situation in which it is not possible to fight a largely technological war, however, they will be in a much more dangerous position. While aristocracy can govern effectively, it is much less adept at commanding the loyalty of the large numbers of people which will be necessary to fight any conventional war. They will have to hand a great deal of power to their military establishments, which traditionally have been far more theocratically inclined than any other technocratic institution. As a result, the overclass will be forced to choose between probable defeat and the empowerment of social forces that threaten their domestic hegemony. This dilemma will, of course, be much easier to resolve in those nations with a strong secular culture. Nonetheless, in countries such as Russia, which is broadly secular but has a powerful church and even more powerful military, the swing toward theocracy in a case of war might be strong enough to effect a change of regime.

This emerging international system, then, will probably not be much different from our own. Democracy has always been a largely domestic affair, most effective with small groups, and attempts to impose it on an international stage have been notable failures.

The real difference will be found within the emerging regimes themselves, in which enormous changes will have taken place with little consultation and, in many cases, without anyone noticing until it's all over. There is a strong likelihood that in many places the change will go unacknowledged for some time. As at the dawn of the Roman Empire, the ancient traditions of the Republic were maintained for decades, even centuries, after they had ceased to be effective or meaningful. In certain places, debate or even violence may break out over a road that has, in fact, already been taken.

This emerging world will be, in many ways, less free than the one in which we currently live, though the freedoms that remain will probably be meaningful and important than many of those we currently enjoy. Certainly, there is a possibility that, at least in the neo-aristocratic regimes, people will be more secure and more prosperous than they are today; while in the theocracies there will be a psychological peace that, while it is based upon illusions, cannot fail to induce a measure of personal happiness.

The open question, perhaps, is what people will do once the masks have been removed and the reality of a new and very different world is undeniable. They may repent and resent the loss of liberal democracy. Some of them may even rise up in valiant, but likely vain, attempts to restore it. Or they may, as Augustus did upon his deathbed, simply say with resignation, "the comedy is over."

Made in the USA
Lexington, KY
23 January 2018